Lovescapes

LOVESCAPES

By
Julia Summers

**Photographs
by
Jim Cozad**

HALLMARK EDITIONS

Copyright © 1971 by Hallmark Cards, Inc.,
Kansas City, Missouri. All Rights Reserved.
Printed in the United States of America.
Library of Congress Catalog Card Number: 74-164661.
Standard Book Number: 87529-232-1.

LOVESCAPES

I can't remember the date
or what you wore
or what the weather was like
on the day we met.
I only remember
that you said hello
in a voice that sounded
like love.

At first
it was hard to say, "I love you."
But my eyes,
my hands,
my silences
kept saying it for me...

...until "I love you"
became the beautiful punctuation
of all our moments together.

Arm in arm
we hurry down the street,
anxious to be alone,
oblivious to the glances
of jealousy and wonder
that recognize
our miracle of love.

When we said goodnight
I ran home with my memories
and sorted them out in my mind.
I stacked them this way and that,
like a child with his blocks...

...and found

that there was

just the right number

to build a quiet room

of love.

The doorways to understanding
can swing wide for us.
They did this afternoon
in the cafe
as we sat and talked
and downed our drug:
two cups of coffee
laced with love.

I didn't know
that love could be this way.
I didn't know that love
could be my food and drink...

...my sun all day,

my dreams at night,

my thoughts,

words,

fears,

hopes...

my joy!

I have a treasure in my purse...
a priceless collection
of ticket stubs,
matchbooks,
notes scrawled on napkins
that remind me of your love....
...To anyone else
they would be worthless
but they are very dear to me...
precious souvenirs
of us.

Everything went wrong today.

Car wouldn't start...

late for work...

an argument with the boss.

It was one of THOSE days
until you met me after work,
turning my day rightside-up
with your smile.

I love the strong you,
encircling my happiness
with your arms.
I love the quiet you,
walking in the rain,
looking into the fire...

I love the childlike you,
bringing me roses
and forgetting the bread...

I love the tender you,
kissing me gently
as we linger
in our private world.
Always.
All the you's,
I love.

Yesterday on the street
I saw someone from the back
and thought he was you.
I ran to him,
calling your name...
...and when he turned,
seeing my surprise
and disappointment,
he looked disappointed, too,
knowing he wasn't the one...
knowing his wasn't the face
that brings me such joy.

I watched you sleeping
so still and serene
beneath the covers....

You were defenseless,
artless, innocent,
like a little child...
and very beautiful.

Do I trust you?
What a silly question.
Of course I trust you
except
sometimes
when you look too long
at a pretty girl...

...sometimes
when you're supposed
to pick me up at seven
and don't arrive
till almost eight...
...sometimes
when you get
that distant look in your eyes
and I feel your thoughts
slipping away from me.

Do I trust you?
Completely! (Almost.)
But without the almost
I probably wouldn't love you
in the first place.

Sometimes you're silly.
You act like a little boy
instead of a grown man...

...guess-whoing me
with your hands over my eyes,
leaving love notes
under pillows and inside books...

...running away from me
and laughing
whenever I act silly
and chase you like a little girl
instead of a grown woman
who is very much in love.

If you should go away
and years
begin to fade the memories,
erasing lines of dialogue,
making vague
the dates and places...

...my lips and skin
will still remember.
My hands
will still know
all the contours...

...and clearly feel
the touch of you.

I'm glad

that we don't have cages

for each other

with locks

and keys

and shrouds at night

to hide us from the stars...

...I'm glad
that we're like singing birds
free to fly away
in search of other songs...

...and eager,

always eager,

to return.

We have a dream of love.
We will look for it
in the hidden places
of the future,
in the secret places
of our hearts.
And if the dream's reality
is never wholly ours
it will not matter...
we will have looked with love...
we will have journeyed in joy!

Set in Devinne, an adaptation of the original roman
face named after T. L. DeVinne.
Typography by Hallmark Photo Composition.
Printed on Hallmark Eggshell Book paper.
Designed by Jay D. Johnson